WHO PUT THE PIZZA IN THE VCR?

Who Put the Pizza in the VCR?

Laughing Your Way Through
Life's Little Emergencies

Martha Bolton

SERVANT PUBLICATIONS
ANN ARBOR, MICHIGAN

Vine Books is an imprint of Servant Publications especially designed to
serve evangelical Christians.

Published by Servant Publications
P.O. Box 8617
Ann Arbor, Michigan 48107

Published in association with the literary agency of Alive Communications,
Inc., P.O. Box 49068, Colorado Springs, Colorado, 80949.

Cover design: Left Coast Design, Inc., Portland, Oregon

96 97 98 99 00 10 9 8 7 6 5 4 3 2

Printed in the United States of America
ISBN 0-89283-958-9

LIBRARY OF CONGRESS CATALOGING-IN-PUBLICATION DATA

Bolton, Martha.
    Who put the pizza in the VCR? : laughing your way through life's little
emergencies / Martha Bolton.
        p.   cm.
    ISBN 0-89283-958-9
    1. Parenthood—Anecdotes. 2. Parenthood—Humor. 3. Toddlers—
Anecdotes. 4. Toddlers—Humor. 5. Infants—Anecdotes. 6. Infants—
Humor. I. Title.
HQ755.8.B65 1996
306.874—dc20   96-30668
                                                          CIP

Dedication

To my aunt and "almost" mother, Agee Stevens

Contents

Acknowledgments

A special thanks to:

My husband, Russ, who couldn't bear to be in the delivery room but has never balked at changing a diaper.

My sons, Russ, Matt, and Tony for all the stories they've given me to work with over the years.

My editor, Heidi Hess, who always kept me on track. (It's amazing how much work a writer can get done handcuffed to a computer!)

And to all of you mothers and fathers of little ones, may this book give you some laughs to help get you through your day. *(You can also sprawl out on the sofa, place it over your face, and make your family think you're asleep!)*

Who Put the Pizza in the VCR?

Humpty Dumpty sat on a wall.
From there he could see a lot.
Like who it was who dropped that worm
Into the coffee pot.

"I'll bet you're wondering how all this sand got in my room, aren't you, Mommy?"

Children are naturally inquisitive. They ask lots of questions. It's how they learn.

Parents have an inquisitive nature, too. They ask lots of questions. It's how *they* learn.

"Who's been playing with the telephone, and why is the operator on the other end of the line speaking German?"

"Who filled Daddy's good shoes with Lime Jell-O?"

"Who dressed the hamster in the Superman costume?"

"Who left the bath water running, and wasn't that Grandma I just saw bodysurfing down the hall?"

"Whose idea was it to recarpet the entire house in wall-to-wall Charmin?"

"Who sprayed the cat with Silly String?"

"Who's taking up modern art and decided to turn our dining room wall into his first canvas?"

"How did the pet snake escape from its cage, and why is Aunt Melva riding the ceiling fan?"

"Who licked all the creamy filling out of that brand-new package of Oreos?" (Judging from the three tooth marks on the cookies, the culprit was either the baby or Uncle Jethro.)

"Who put Mommy's favorite Passion Fruit Punch nail polish on Chipper's paws?"

And, of course, the question that all parents ask sooner or later—"Who put the pizza in the VCR?"

Is There a Baby in the House?

Walking through a maze of toys
Like a laboratory mouse?
Got bags under both your eyes?
There's a *baby* in the house!

Whenever my husband and I are invited to another couple's home for dinner, we can usually tell without even asking whether or not there are children in the house. You can learn to do this, too. All you have to do is look for one or more of these telltale signs.

You Know There's a Baby in the House When...

- The only dinner music they're playing is "Barney's Greatest Hits."

- A bib is part of your place setting.

- They're serving teething biscuits instead of dinner rolls.

- The hostess offers you your beverage in a Sit 'n' Sip cup.

- All the eating utensils are rubber coated with Mickey Mouse handles.

- They're using Baby Wipes for napkins.

- The host offers to purée everyone's meat for them.

- The gravy has the distinct taste of formula.

- When the hostess offers you dessert, she spells it.

- The only accessories the hostess is wearing are a burp diaper on her left shoulder and a pacifier on a string around her neck.

But you *really* know there's a baby in the house when the host and hostess start yawning at seven-thirty, and are face down in their mashed potatoes by eight!

Vive la Difference

A weight gain after Baby?
Don't fret… you'll lose it all
With all the chasing that you'll do
Once Baby learns to crawl.

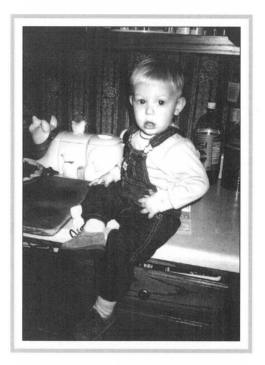

"Brownies? What brownies?
I didn't see any brownies!"

As your baby grows older, you'll quickly discover there is a world of difference between living in a house with infants and living in a house with toddlers. Some of those differences are obvious, such as those portable gates and safety latches you have to install around the house when toddlers are around. There are other changes that take place in your life, too. For instance:

- A baby likes to play peek-a-boo. A toddler prefers playing hide-and-seek... with your car keys.

- A baby usually won't complain when you dress her. A toddler considers pulling a turtleneck over her head "cruel and unusual" punishment.

- When Uncle Bill and Aunt Ruth gave your baby a beautiful bassinet for your shower, you wondered how you could ever thank them enough. When this same lovely couple gives your toddler a toy drum set for his first birthday, you'll wonder how you can ever *get even!*

- If a baby wants to eat at two o'clock in the morning, he cries for Mom. If a toddler wants to eat at two o'clock in the morning, he cries for Ronald McDonald.

- When nature calls, Baby gets his diapers changed and you can continue with your day. A toddler sits on the potty chair and has to go through twenty-three rounds of E-I-E-I-O before she confesses she was too late for the potty chair in the first place.

- Every time Baby sits, you coax him into showing off his new skill—crawling. But you spend so much time and energy picking up after your toddler that every time he crawls, you coax him into showing off his old skill—sitting still.

- If a baby's quiet, you leave him be. If a toddler's quiet, better go and see!

- A baby loves to go shopping, and will probably lie quietly in his stroller. A toddler loves to go shopping, and will probably want to get out and push his stroller... into the nearest stack of canned goods.

If you were to take a survey, though, I'm sure the most cherished difference would be this:

A baby receives hugs and kisses.
A toddler can give them back.

Combat Duty

Hickory, Dickory, Dock
The sitter watched the clock.
Tied to a chair
By that sweet little dear.
Hickory, Dickory, Dock.

Babysitters. They've endured it all—from pet snakes on the loose to "burned at the stake" reenactments. For some of them, Desert Storm would have been a vacation.

Their calling is a noble one. Frankly, I never could have made it without my babysitters (several of whom are now living at Shaky Palms Home for the Nervous). As good as they were, though, I wonder how they would have fared in today's world of childcare providers.

In my day, when Mom and Dad wanted to go out for an evening alone, all they had to do was hire a sitter and leave the number where they could be reached. The instructions parents have to leave behind today are far more complex:

Babysitter Instructions

If you need us, we'll be at 555-6493. Or you can beep us on our pager at 555-3216. Or call us on our cell phone at 555-2589. Or E-mail us at Mom/Dad.SOS.com. If you *still* can't reach us, walk next door. We're spending the evening with the neighbors.

If Baby's pacifier thermometer indicates her temperature is elevated, recheck it with her headband thermometer. Should that show a fever, too, see if her bracelet thermometer agrees. If it does, her thermometer pajamas should change colors as well. If they have, verify with the digital thermometer and administer ibuprofen.

When you change Baby, be sure to use the pink diapers. The blue ones are for her brother. Don't use the yellow ones either (they're for Easter), or the red and green ones (they're for Christmas). The ones with the palm tree design are for summer, so don't use them yet. And don't use the ones with hearts. They're strictly for February. The black-trimmed ones are for formal wear, and the red, white, and blue ones are for the Fourth of July. If there are no pink ones, then go ahead and use a white one. But for goodness' sake, *not after Labor Day!*

Feed Baby at precisely 8:00. The timer should go off in her crib, which you'll be able to hear over her nursery monitor. Give her the Puréed Quiche. If she spits that out, try the Tofu Broth. If she tosses that across the room, let her sample the Strained Liver Pâté. If she tosses *you* across the room, just give her her bottle.

If Baby appears to be fighting sleep, put Heartbeat Bunny in bed with her. It's a stuffed bunny that has the soothing sounds of Mother's heartbeat. If that doesn't work, try Sneezing Lamb. It sounds like Mother during allergy season. If that doesn't help, try Stomach Growling Lion. It sounds like Daddy between meals. Snoring Bear sounds like Grandpa, and the Whimpering Puppies sound like Mom and Dad during tax season. If none of these work, go back to Heartbeat Bunny. At least *he* won't wake up the neighbors!

If Baby acts bored or fussy, let her watch television. If that doesn't work, try putting on one of her favorite videos. If she doesn't go for that, let her play computer games on her laptop. If that doesn't interest her, give her ten minutes on the Internet. If she's *still* fussy, try her Game Boy, her Sega, or her library of books on tape. If all else fails, try *talking* to her. Maybe... just maybe... she just wants some company.

Sleepless in the Nursery

Rock-a-bye baby
On the tree top.
Please get to sleep or
Your parents will drop!

When there's a baby in the house, it's not always easy to get a full eight hours of sleep. Usually you have to catch a nap wherever and whenever you can. If there's more than one child in the house, the situation is even more complicated. No sooner do you get one youngster to sleep than the other one wakes up.

Instead of battling constant fatigue, try looking for creative places to catch up on your much-needed rest. Here are a few of my favorites:

In your closet. For maximum relaxation, suspend your bathrobe between two hangers and use as a hammock.

In the bathtub. Go ahead and let Calgon take you away. (Getting a full eight hours this way is not recommended, however—unless you're planning to iron out your skin later.)

In line at the DMV. If you close your eyes whenever the car registration line comes to a dead standstill, chances are you'll get in a good twenty minute nap before the line starts moving again.

At a restaurant. Take the booth in the farthest corner, put a few cucumber slices over your eyes, then use the tablecloth for a blanket. (Be careful to remove lit candle first.)

While stopped at a red light. Three-way intersections work the best. One word of caution, though—sprawling out on the hood might create a scene and cause unnecessary panic.

On top of your washing machine. Depending on the location of your laundry room, it could take an hour or more before somebody finds you. (You'll also get a great massage every time the spin cycle rolls around.)

At a Little League game. Be careful not to yawn at the precise moment a fly ball is headed in your direction... unless you've got sufficient dental coverage.

At a car wash. Apply your brakes during the scrub cycle and those giant brushes will shield you from being seen by anyone. You'll get in a restful nap while workers spend the next several hours trying to locate the problem.

At church. If the cribs in the nursery are filled (and too small for you anyway), then try hiding behind your hymnal to get a few short winks during the church announcements. (But first make sure you're not the one who's supposed to be *making* those announcements.)

On the copy machine at work. Not only will this give you some much needed rest, but you can use the copier to make several low-tech clones of yourself to help you get all your work done.

On the beach. Be sure to awaken before high tide... unless you're planning on taking that long-awaited vacation overseas the hard way.

In a shopping cart at the grocery store. Why not make the kids push *you* for a change? (Using a frozen turkey as a pillow, however, could leave your nose with a severe case of frostbite.)

But the best place to sleep is...

In the mattress section of your local department store. But be sure to wake up before closing time, or they can legally charge you rent!

He Ain't Heavy, He's My Baby

Little Jack Horner
Sat in a corner
Because he was feeling quite stiff.
Poor Little Jack
Threw out his back
From the diaper bag he tried to lift!

Parenting isn't for the weak—especially when it comes to hauling around the minimum daily requirement of baby equipment.

Diaper bags. I wouldn't be surprised if one day Diaper Bag Lifting becomes an Olympic event. Body builders may impress the world now by lifting 200, 300, even 400 pounds. But let them work their way up to a diaper bag on each side of the bar—then we'll really see those neck veins pop out!

For most people, lifting the average diaper bag requires a back brace and a body building course. It wouldn't hurt to have an orthopedic surgeon on stand-by, too. Frankly, I don't see how a plastic satchel that's lighter than air when empty can feel like an anvil by merely adding a few bottles of formula, some diapers, and a box of Baby Wipes. But it does. Some bags get so heavy, they should be checked in at highway weigh stations.

Strollers. Many people are under the mistaken assumption that *anyone* can operate a stroller. It's as if they think all they have to do is place Baby inside the stroller and start pushing. This couldn't be further from the truth.

Anyone who has ever walked in front of a tailgating stroller would agree that only licensed stroller operators should be allowed behind the handle of these heel chasers. Additionally, turn signals, brake lights, and a horn (one that automatically beeps whenever the stroller is shifted into reverse) should be standard equipment.

Of course, there are finer points of stroller training as well. Folding and unfolding the stroller, for example. Emergency workers across the nation can cite case after case of parents needing to be surgically untangled from their child's stroller. One poor dad in Phoenix could only be freed using the Jaws of Life.

High chairs and miscellaneous babyware. The high chair has its own set of problems. There's no telling how many children have had to be pushed across the stage in their high chairs to receive their high-school diplomas simply because a caregiver with no formal high-chair training couldn't get the tray unstuck.

Add to that the aggravation of car seats, playpens, infant carriers, and baby swings, and it's no wonder Maalox sales among young parents are going through the roof.

But don't despair. It does get easier with time. Children grow up, and they start carrying *your* things. First it's your spare change, then they graduate to your car keys. By the time the college years roll around, you'll have to nail the furniture to the floor in order to keep it from walking away, too!

Tears on My Pillow

Hush, little Baby
Don't you cry.
You don't pay the bills.
It's your mother and I.

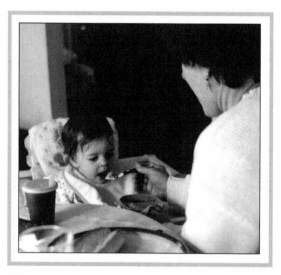

"If Mom's making all those
yummy sounds, why doesn't
she eat this stuff?"

Trying to figure out why Baby is crying can be frustrating. Why are his lips pouting? Why are those precious tears flowing down his little cheeks? Why are his delicate wails vibrating the windows and breaking all the crystal within a three-mile radius?

Hopefully, the following checklist will help parents better determine the origin of their baby's temporary discomfort.

Top Ten Reasons
Why Baby Might Be Crying

10. He's hungry.
 9. He's wet.
 8. He needs to be burped.
 7. He's teething.
 6. He's sick.
 5. He's wet again.
 4. He's noticed there are twelve more jars of puréed liver left in the cabinet.
 3. He definitely does not like the bunny outfit with the ears and tail that Aunt Beulah just brought over for him.
 2. Someone moved his playpen in front of the television set, and this is the third talk show in a row that he's had to sit through.
 1. Baby saw Daddy crying after he caught a glimpse of the hospital bill, and decided to join him.

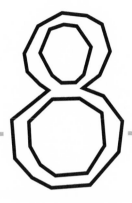

A Change for the Better

When checking Baby's diaper,
It really would be wise
To never slide your finger in—
You might get a surprise!

Whether you use a diaper service or buy disposables, diapers can get awfully expensive. Our Three-Baby Diaper Brigade prompted us to buy our diapers by the case. We'd special order them from our local department store, then drive to the merchandise loading dock every week or so to pick up the three-by-four-foot box of diapers.

Of course, we might not have needed so many had we not wasted them by breaking the adhesive tabs to check the diapers before they were actually soiled. But then, when we checked it the other way (by slipping our finger through the side of the diaper), well... you know the rest of *that* story.

Remembering mishaps such as these has prompted me to provide parents with the following Diaper Changing Guide.

You Know It's Time to Change the Diaper When...

- It's sagging more than the economy.

- Baby's favorite crib toy is a gas mask.

- The wallpaper in the nursery is starting to peel.

- The cat's litter box has suddenly become the most fragrant part of the house.

- No one can smell the liver and onions you're cooking for dinner.

- Your neighbors on each side of you put their houses up for sale... under market.

- Your parrot has started saying, "Polly wants some air freshener."

- Stray dogs skip your lawn. They figure you already put up with enough.

- You pick up Baby and get your *second* shower of the day.

- The animals on Baby's crib mobile quit going around in circles and head for the door.

- Baby's first words are, "Can somebody open a window?"

- The fish in your aquarium are gasping for oxygen.

- You notice door-to-door salesmen are passing by your house.

- The family dog brings in the paper and opens it to an ad for fumigation.

But you really know it's time to change the diaper when you changed the last one less than two minutes ago. There's just something about a brand new diaper that seems to make babies want to break it in right away.

All Washed Up

Rub a dub dub.
Baby, get in that tub!
You prob'ly don't care
But dirt's not formalwear!

Most babies love to play in water. That's how they started out, so I suppose it just feels natural to them. There are, though, some important things a parent should be aware of concerning Baby's nightly bath. Note the following:

- After ten seconds in the water, Baby becomes slippery and is as difficult to hold on to as a twenty-pound trout.

- Baby usually enjoys playing with several bath toys (i.e., rubber ducky, toy boats, miniature submarines)... provided Dad isn't busy playing with them elsewhere in the house.

- Bath water should be lukewarm. It shouldn't be cold enough to drink (although Baby is sure to try doing so), and it should never be too hot. There will be plenty of time in the adolescent and teenage years for Baby to get *herself* into hot water.

- Due to the danger of slipping, Baby should never stand up in the bathtub—unless, of course, she's giving her annual State of the Family address, in which case appropriate swimwear should be worn.

- Never leave the room while Baby is in the bathtub. It's the only way to ensure her safety. (If Baby is a splasher, you might want to sit within splashing distance and get your own bath out of the way at the same time.)

• Watch for signs that Baby is ready to get out of the bathtub. These might include, but are not limited to: unplugging the drain, trying to climb out on her own, spelling out "S.O.S." in the suds, putting a "rescue me" note in a bottle floating in your direction....

And finally, after drying Baby, remember to use baby powder for that silky smooth feeling. (But avoid the temptation to use the entire canister unless your bathroom is equipped with an advanced radar system to maneuver you through the dense clouds and safely out the door.)

10

Designer Babies

There was an old woman who lived in a shoe.
Her home was run down, and she needed to move.
So she saved and she saved and she got a great deal
On an Air Jordan high-top with a pump-up heel!

"But, Mom, I *do* have my sweater on!"

I needed to buy a shower gift the other day, so I walked into a store and asked the clerk where their baby clothes were.

"Guess?" she replied.

"I don't have time to guess," I told her. "Can't you just tell me where they are?"

"No," she laughed. "I mean, do you want Guess or Christian Dior?"

"I'm shopping for a *baby*," I repeated, figuring she had misunderstood me.

"How 'bout Calvin Klein?" she continued.

"Calvin Klein?" I asked. "She's just a baby. Don't you have any *regular* baby clothes?"

"You mean generic baby wear?" she gasped in disbelief.

"Yeah. Where would I find that?"

"In the 1970's," she said, then went on to wait on another customer.

Designer labels. Wasn't it enough pressure when our teenagers had to have name brand clothing? Now, it's the toddler set.

Frankly, I don't get it. Why do babies need designer jeans? Are they afraid they'll end up on Mr. Blackwell's Worst Dressed Toddler List? And why would a baby *need* $100 running shoes? For better ankle support for when she's jogging from one end of the crib to the other?

So what if a child is clothed from the most exclusive

line of clothing that money can buy? After it's been burped on, wet in, and spilled on a dozen or so times, does it really matter whose logo is getting further stained with the puréed green peas?

When I was growing up, HMD was the major label (Hand Me Down). It was a different kind of Guess clothing. Everyone had to *guess* whose outfit it used to be. And just like the ad promised, I outgrew all my Carters before they wore out. But I *still* had to wear them. One T-shirt was so snug, my arms swelled up like Popeye's every time I put it on. I was wearing miniskirts long before they were in style, and when a blouse didn't fit, my mother would try to convince me that the cuffs were made to stop at the elbow. The very first words I ever spoke were, "Are we expecting a flood—or is it just these pants?"

Don't get me wrong. I'm not saying there's anything wrong with designer wear. I've bought my share of it, too. But babies look cute in *anything*—whether it's an HMD or an outfit direct from Rodeo Drive. Why worry about whether or not their clothes are flattering to their figure, or whether the color is in their "season," or if another baby is going to show up at pre-school wearing the exact same outfit? Who they are is far more important than who they wear.

11

Baby-U

Happy Birthday, Baby!
Today, you're turning one!
But you can't open presents
'Til your calculus is done!

"I want that report on my desk by the end of the day or you're outta here!"

The only parent who can truthfully say his child is perfect is God. Yet, from time to time, you'll run into one of *"them"*—those parents who are convinced their offspring have the I.Q. of Einstein, the looks of Tom Cruise, the athletic potential of Joe Montana, and the talent of the Three Tenors all rolled into one. Those parents have a knack for making you feel inferior if your child can't speak six languages by his first birthday and isn't on Jeopardy by the time he turns three.

I recall an encounter I once had. It took place in a park, and if my memory serves me correctly, it went something like this:

"What a cute baby," the woman commented as she parked her stroller next to mine.

"Thank you," I smiled. "Yours, too."

"Yes, he is, isn't he?" she beamed, releasing Junior to play.

"How old is he?" I asked, noticing the briefcase in which he transported his toys.

"Eighteen months," she replied. "And yours?"

"He just had his second birthday last week."

"What's he taking?"

"Nothing," I shot back, slightly offended. "That toy is *his.*"

"No," the lady said. "I mean, what *courses* is he taking? You know, to get ready for college."

"He's only two. He's not even in preschool yet."

"Are you saying your child isn't receiving any specialized training at all?" she gasped.

"Right now just 'potty.'"

"Think of the years you've wasted already."

"I haven't wasted any years," I insisted. "We play, we go for walks, I'm teaching him his alphabet."

"What about his SAT's?"

"They're part of the alphabet."

"Look, maybe it's not too late. Perhaps you could sign him up for some correspondence courses. You can teach him at home. Has he decided on his major yet?"

"He hasn't really said," I answered, playing along. "Maybe dentistry. He's been spending a lot of time with his teething ring lately."

"Dentistry? All the more reason that he should have a head start on his academics."

"I'll look into it," I smiled, in a discreet attempt to slide out of the conversation.

"But academics aren't everything," she continued, not letting me slide very far. "There are the arts, too. Have you exposed your son to the music of the great composers?"

"If you wind up his teddy bear, it plays 'Three Blind Mice.'"

"I assume it's safe to say you haven't started him on a musical instrument either."

"He's only two!" I protested. "Lifting a tuba now could give him a hernia."

"Look," she bragged, "our son is younger than yours and already he's quite skillful with the violin."

"I can see that. He's over there using it as a bucket in that sandbox."

"Junior!" she snapped, jumping to her feet. "Empty out that violin right now! You've got a recital in an hour!"

Junior proceeded to empty the violin, she grabbed his hand, and marched off with him. "And then there's your swim lesson, your polo lesson, your dance class, your art instruction, your gymnastics class, your creative writing seminar...."

As their silhouettes began to fade into the distance, I paused long enough to wonder if maybe I *was* wasting time. Maybe we *should* fill every moment of our child's day with extracurricular activities and calculus tutors. But as I watched my son playing, as I heard his laughter, I decided instead to simply slow down and enjoy the day, the park—and my son's childhood—a little longer.

Labor Wars

My labor was far worse than yours was.
The pains didn't let up, not once!
My labor was far worse than yours was.
It lasted for twenty-four months!

Have you ever had the misfortune to be around one of those mothers who are convinced *theirs* was the longest and most painful labor in history? No matter what yours was like, theirs was worse. If yours required two obstetricians, theirs required the entire hospital staff, plus the casts of "E.R." *and* "Chicago Hope." I ran into one of these mothers the other day.

"*My* labor lasted *three* days," she said, still cringing from the memory even though it had been decades ago.

Three days? Big deal, I thought to myself. *Mine* lasted a week! Or was it *two?*

"My screams could be heard throughout the entire maternity ward!" she added.

I could have told her that *my* screams were picked up by overhead aircraft, but figuring she wouldn't hear me anyway, I simply kept my comments to myself.

"I retained more water than the average pregnancy," she continued.

I retained more water than the Hoover Dam!

"I gained so much weight, I outgrew all my maternity clothes," she added.

I gained so much weight, I outgrew all my doorways!

"I've got stretch marks over twenty percent of my body."

Even my stretch marks have stretch marks!

"During labor, I kept my mind off the excruciating pain by coming up with names I could call the baby."

During labor, I kept my mind off the excruciating pain by coming up with names I could call my husband!

"I told my doctor I wanted to be awake for the entire birth."

I told my doctor not to wake me until Baby's first year of college!

"My baby weighed nine pounds, four ounces at birth."

I don't know how big my baby was at birth. He walked out and got in the car before anyone could weigh him.

The main problem with mothers who exaggerate their birthing stories like this is that they make it that much more difficult for the rest of us to stretch the truth!

What's Up, Doc?

Baby was due for her two-year exam,
So I called up the doc on the phone.
I drove to his office and waited our turn.
But by the time she was called... she was grown!

Having a baby in your life can hardly ever be described as boring. Except maybe when you're waiting in an examination room for the doctor.

There's not a whole lot to do while waiting in an examination room. Once you've cut off the circulation in your arm with the blood pressure cuff and guessed the correct number of tongue depressors and bandaids in the little jars, what else is there to do?

I used to think the same thing, but now I've come up with the following tips to help parents combat Examination Room Boredom.

Things to Do While Waiting for the Pediatrician

- Take Baby's temperature. Take your temperature. Take the temperature of that ice cold stethoscope the doctor always uses.

- Weigh Baby. Weigh your purse. Discover that Baby is four pounds lighter than your purse.

- Using the doctor's suture kit, sew up the backs of all the examination gowns.

- Write down the names of all universities listed on the degrees decorating the wall. You can call and verify these later. If you find one from "Betty's School of Beauty and Medicine," however, you might wish to consider changing doctors.

• Rehang crooked pictures in examination room using the doctor's reflex hammer.

• Use the jar of Q-tips for their intended purpose.

• Use the jar of Q-tips for non-intended purposes (to play Pick-Up Sticks, to build a replica of the White House, to do your walrus impersonation).

• Play Bumper Cars with the doctor's stool on wheels. (Going out into the hallways to play with the other parents is not recommended—unless one of the nurses is available to referee.)

And finally, see how many different ways you can adjust the examination table. (But be careful not to fold yourself up inside it. One poor dad did this, and they didn't find him for 3 years.)

A Matter of Record

Mother had a little book
In which she wrote each day
About her little baby
And the cute things he would say.
She wrote about his first steps,
And what he wants to be.
And if it's ever published,
He wants a royalty!

Baby books are great because they help parents keep an accurate record of important dates and facts regarding their child's development.

Most parents have every intention of filling in each and every page of their baby's memory book. For the first child, they probably do a good job of that. By Child #2, the parent is already well into the hustle-bustle of parenting, and may only get as far as The Toddler Years in his book. Child #3? Well, in some instances, he's lucky if his *name* makes it in!

Of course, Mom and Dad are every bit as proud of each child, and love them all equally. It's just that the more children there are in the house, the less time a parent tends to have for these things. Consequently, the baby books of three siblings could end up reading something like this:

First Child's Book	Name: Sara Ann
Second Child's Book	Name: Mary Beth
Third Child's Book	Name: Sara Ann Mary Beth Cindy Sue

(Children of large families are often called by their siblings' names first. The more upset the parent is, the longer it will take them to run through all the names to get to the right one. If the parent is *really* mad, a few of the cousins' names, neighbor's names, and the Brady Bunch slip in, too.)

First Child's Book	Born: January 16, 1985
Second Child's Book	Born: March 1987
Third Child's Book	Born: Sometime in the fall 1989

First Child's Book	Weight: 8.129458 lbs.
Second Child's Book	Weight: 7 lbs. 4 ozs.
Third Child's Book	Weight: between 5 to 12 lbs.

First Child's Book	Time in Labor: 17 hours
Second Child's Book	Time in Labor: 8 hours
Third Child's Book	Time in Labor: 15 minutes (stopped by hospital to give birth on way to grocery store)

First Child's Book	First words: Mommy, Daddy, bye-bye, bottle, NaNa, uh-oh, baby
Second Child's Book	First words: go, no, oh, toy
Third Child's Book	First words: Probably English

First Child's Book	Favorite foods: Anything sugar-free, fat-free, cholesterol free, lactose-free, 100% natural, and organically grown
Second Child's Book	Favorite foods: Anything fat-free and 75% natural
Third Child's Book	Favorite foods: Anything dirt-free

First Child's Book	First tooth to fall out: 10-7-91 (left $5 under pillow)
Second Child's Book	First tooth to fall out: 5-1-93 (left $3 under pillow)

Third Child's Book	First tooth to fall out: 6-13-95 (left IOU under pillow—have priced braces)

First Child's Book	Favorite clothing: dress with red skirt, white top and matching jacket
Second Child's Book	Favorite clothing: hand-me-down dress with red skirt and white top. Jacket missing.
Third Child's Book	Favorite clothing: hand-me-down dress with red skirt and pink top (accidentally washed red skirt and white top together in hot water)

First Child's Book	First day of school: 9-12-90 (Mommy cried all day. I can't believe you're growing up so fast.)
Second Child's Book	First day of school: 9-10-92 (I can't believe it's that time again already. I'm going to miss you kids, but I can sure use the rest.)
Third Child's Book	First day of school: 9-12-94 (But we arrived at school on 8-30-94 and waited for gates to open.)

Picture This

Got a coupon in the mail,
But I had to just ignore it.
Through the years I've learned one thing—
If it's free, I can't *afford* it!

"Say 'Cheese'? I don't even *like* cheese!"

The offer was clear—"one free 8 x 10 portrait of your baby." What a deal! All I had to do was bring my baby for the sitting, have him smile for the photographer, choose our proof, and pick up our free photo. Right?

Life is never that simple.

"You're absolutely going to *love* these pictures of your little angel," the photographer gushed as he led me to the order table. I braced myself, determined to get away with my free photo and nothing more. I just hoped my resolve wouldn't weaken once I saw all those irresistible poses.

"This first one is my favorite." The photographer pointed to the first proof on his computer screen. "What do you think?" he asked, proudly.

"It's nice," I said. "But one of his eyes is closed."

"That's what makes the picture soooooo unique," he beamed. "You see, this side shows what your baby looks like *awake*. And this side shows what your baby looks like *asleep*. Two looks, one picture. You like? No?"

I shook my head.

"Well, then, what about this one?" he asked, bringing the next photo up on the screen.

"He's falling out of the shot," I pointed out.

"The untrained eye would see a baby falling out of the shot. But I see a picture that says *childhood—how quickly it goes away.*"

"How much would a four-by-six of that one be?" I asked.

"Thirty-six dollars."

"Thirty-six dollars?" I repeated in disbelief. "I see a picture that says *my paycheck—how quickly it goes away.*"

He moved on to the next shot.

"You've *got* to love this one," he said.

"It's a little dark, don't you think?"

"I call it, 'Evening in the Nursery,'" he beamed.

"I'd call it 'Camera with the Lens Cap On.'"

The photographer and I were both growing more and more frustrated by the minute.

"This is my *last* picture. It's clear. The colors are vivid. It's perfect," he said, moving to the final proof.

"Well, it *would* be perfect, if it were of my child," I said.

"It *is* your child. He's to the right of the other little boy. It's a double exposure, but it *still works.*"

Endeavoring to be as delicate as possible, I just *had* to say it.

"Didn't you take any *good* pictures?"

"Good, ma'am, is a matter of artistic taste," the photographer huffed, snapping off the light illuminating the photographs. "And you, apparently, do not appreciate fine art. I shall now bid you *good day!*"

"But what about my free 8 x 10?" I asked.

"I thought you didn't like these photos."

"I don't," I said. "But I figure if I take the one with one eye closed and one eye open and save it until he turns sixteen, it'll sure make him appreciate his driver's license picture!"

Tell Me Something I Don't Know

I learned about diaper rash,
And nursing dont's and do's.
But how come no one warned me
'Bout those "terrible twos"?

Some day your kid is going to come up to you, look you straight in the eye, and ask why he has to learn so much useless stuff in school.

When that day comes, it might be a good idea if you had a little ammunition under your belt. If you think about it, there are things you learned in school that you never thought would come in handy in life, but they did—especially with parenting!

My high-school sewing class taught me how to sew a blouse (mine ended up with two extra sleeves), how to make a gym bag (the only thing I forgot was the opening), and how to hem a skirt (I used staples). But what little I learned helped me when it came time to make that rutabaga costume for my son's preschool Food Group Talent Show. It also got me through those Huey, Duey, and Louie costumes I made for a fall costume party (I used yellow Playtex Living Gloves for their webbed feet), and the angel outfits I made for the annual Christmas pageant. (The wings kept falling off, and the halos fit more like hula hoops, but they still worked!)

My cooking class taught me how to make my own teething rings (my biscuits could bring any molar to the surface). And my limited knowledge of botany helped me to identify some of the mysterious vegetation covering half-eaten candy bars under my children's beds, or the life forms growing on the floors of their bedroom closets.

Gym class got me in shape for chasing a three-year-old around the house to get him to take his medicine. And thanks to those cars I dodged in driver's education classes, I know how to get out of the way of a Big Wheel.

When you get down to it, though, much of parenting is a "learn as you go" situation. We repeatedly amaze ourselves with how much we know instinctively. Sure, we make our share of mistakes, but as we learned in school, being there and doing our best are the most important requirements.

Language
Barriers

I can speak four languages.
That may come as quite a shock—
English and Pig Latin,
Valley Girl, and Baby Talk!

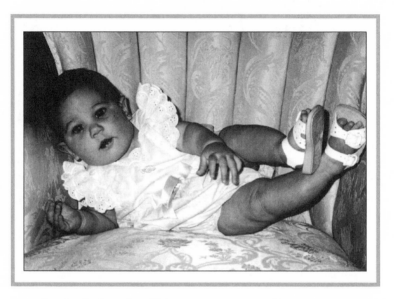

"Let's do lunch. I'll have my mom call your mom."

When my children were little, I used to get together with a group of other young mothers for a time of adult conversation. By "adult" I don't mean "x-rated." I mean engaging in discussions requiring words with more than one syllable.

Grown-ups spending too much time around toddlers can begin to lose their command of the English language. When this happens, take two dictionaries and call the doctor in the morning. At the supermarket I once overheard several young mothers who had evidently succombed to "toddler tongue." Their conversation went something like this:

"Hey, you look terrific! But here... let me wipe off your chin.... There, that's better."

"So, what have you been up to lately... (pinching cheek) besides growing up into a little lady?"

"*You* should talk. How old are you now?"

(Holding up fingers and flashing all ten of them three times.) "This many."

"My, my. You're getting to be such a BIG girl. Can you say 'bi-i-i-i-g girl?'"

"I can dress myself."

"I can tie my shoes."

"I know all my multiplication tables."

"Do not."

"Do, too."

"Do not."

"I'm an accountant! I do, too! And what about you? Did you ever finish your doctorate?"

"Got my diploma last summer. It's hanging on the refrigerator."

There was a lull in the conversation as we all tried to remember the last time we had read a book that wasn't a pop-up, gone out to a restaurant that didn't have a clown maitre d', or heard an eardrum-piercing high "C" note being hit by an entertainer instead of an eight-month-old.

We decided then and there that we all needed to get out more, to see the world, to expand our horizons... right after one more episode of "Sesame Street."

18

Never-Never Land

They say we learn from our mistakes,
And if that's really so,
I'm the world's foremost authority!
There's nothing I don't know!

New parents quickly learn there are a few things they should *never* do. Like forgetting to use the burp cloth over your best suit after Baby downs eight ounces of milk in four seconds flat. Or letting Baby play on your computer before saving the sixty-page manuscript on which you are working.

Lessons such as the above can be learned over time. But new moms and dads might want to keep handy this little list of things I've learned—through painful experience—that parents should never *ever* do.

- Never coax Baby to eat his puréed liver and spinach entree by sampling it yourself.

- Never forget to secure nipple before vigorously shaking bottle.

- Never discuss your in-laws in front of a baby who's just learning to repeat sentences verbatim.

- Never permit Baby to turn on every musical toy in his room simultaneously... unless you own stock in Bayer.

- Never allow Baby to play with your business telephone line... especially if your automatic dialing system has been programmed to three numbers in Japan, two in Argentina, and one in Paris.

- Never powder Baby after saturating her in baby oil, unless you're planning on saving the surplus mixture to make her first Plaster of Paris mold for kindergarten.

- Never borrow from your child's college fund unless you're reasonably sure you can glue all the pieces of the piggy bank together again.

- If entertaining your boss for dinner, never seat him or her in the chair directly across from Baby... especially if you notice Baby making a catapult with his spoon and fork.

- Never let Baby play with the television remote control. That is *Daddy's* toy.

- Never, *ever* miss naptime. And if Baby wants to take one, too, let him.

- And finally, never allow Baby to spit out his dinner. It makes your dinner guests think they have that option, too.

Another Fine Mess

Oh, oh, get me down!
I'm dizzy and I'm pale.
Why did I listen to my kids
And ride this carousel?!

"I thought you said the surf was up!"

I remember my seventy-year-old grandmother crawling in and out of the caves on Tom Sawyer Island at Disneyland. She even got stuck in one of the narrow passageways, just to keep up with her grandchildren.

In his sixties, my father rode several roller coasters in a row with his grandchildren at Knotts' Berry Farm, and ended up spending the rest of the afternoon in the park infirmary.

When he was in his forties, my brother dressed up as Spiderman and jumped from our patio roof in the middle of a birthday party celebration, just so his nephew would think the "real" Spiderman came to his party. It took two weeks for my brother's back to return to normal.

Ah... the things we do for kids.

Through the years, parents, grandparents, uncles, aunts, cousins, and friends have gotten themselves into one fine mess after another simply trying to keep youngsters entertained. We've eaten at far more fast food restaurants than our veins were intended to tolerate. We've lived under the same roof as pet snakes and baby rats. We've watched 4,836 hours of Sesame Street, learning more about the letter "K" than we ever wanted to know. We've let these little angels paint our fingernails and toenails purple, and put lipstick on our eyebrows. We've hopped with them in potato sack races, and have gone with them down quarter-mile water slides.

I once played a T-ball game in semi-formal attire because the scheduled opposing team was a "no show." I had stopped by the game on my way to a banquet when the coach asked the parents if they would mind playing a game against the kids. Not wanting to disappoint the children, we all agreed. I ended up going to the banquet with five runs to my credit—two in the game and three in my nylons.

I've gone fishing even though I can't fish (the only scaly thing I ever bring home is poison ivy), and camping even though I'm no camper (when I rub two sticks together all I get is splinters).

But even with all the messes that kids get us into, even if we pull a ligament here or sprain an ankle there trying to keep up with them, one thing's for certain— they sure do keep our hearts young.

Home Safe

Little Boy Blue,
Get down from there!
You should not be swinging
From that chandelier!

"… and for my *next* escape…"

A baby's first steps are cautious and slow. It's those steps that follow that are so hard to keep up with! When Baby begins to walk, a whole new world opens up to him. He can now go where no infant has gone before, and where parents fear to follow. Because of this, it becomes necessary for parents to "baby-proof" their home.

This usually includes installing safety locks on all the cupboards (especially those which contain hazardous material), adding security handles to all exterior door knobs to prevent Baby from opening the door and going on a cross country hike, and inserting guards on every electric socket in the house. But even that may not go far enough. Some parents (of particularly energetic children) might wish to consider a few extra safeguards:

- Install an automatic shut-off valve in the toilet that would immediately cancel any flush where a toy or tennis ball is involved.

- Set up a network of surveillance cameras to provide instant replay proof of any mischievous behavior. No longer would parents have to wonder who it was who gave the cat a mohawk or dressed the dog in the Elvis outfit. One camera should also be positioned under the dining room table to furnish ample evidence as to which child it is who starts that nightly "kicking under the table."

- No house is properly baby-proofed without the installation of "under the bed" alarms. These would be set to sound off whenever a food item has been hidden under the bed for more than three weeks. (It should be noted that pizzas discovered under the bed can double as hubcaps in a pinch.)

- Beeper Diapers also come in handy when baby-proofing your home. Beeper Diapers are perfect for those times when Junior tries to hide from Mom and Dad. After Mom and Dad have looked everywhere for Junior, all they need to do is dial the assigned number on their telephone, and wait for the diapers to emit a beeping noise. They can then follow the beeping noise to immediately locate Baby.

- Speaking of diapers, a "wetness alarm" would be a handy invention, too. This would sound off whenever the diaper reaches its maximum capacity.

- Fit the cookie jar with the Club locking device, and fit all toilet paper rolls with tracing devices to locate the beginning of the roll without having to follow the trail.

- Scotchgard all carpeting, and cover all upholstery, fine furniture, and visiting relatives in plastic. It's also wise to spray the bottom three feet of all interior walls with crayon repellent.

The best way to baby-proof your home, though, is to remind yourself that all material things are replaceable. Childhood isn't.

What Goes
Up Must
Come Down

There's an old saying
That has always inspired.
Three little words…
"No assembly required!"

I will never forget the Christmas we bought our sons a new swing set. My husband stayed up all night Christmas Eve putting it together. It would have gone faster, but he insisted on doing it the hard way—by reading the "easy to assemble" directions. The directions were about twenty-five pages long, and written in four different languages (none of them English).

The only set of instructions that bore a faint resemblance to our native tongue read as follows: "Insert A into C, bypass B until Step #4, then connect G-1 to D-4, bringing Fig. 8 into alignment with J-7 and overlapping M-3 and P-6. Adjust R-5 to compensate for the 6H4 adjustment."

Since it was too late in the evening to hire an interpreter, my husband tried to decipher the hieroglyphics as best he could.

He wasn't totally lost, though, because he had *me*. Men *need* their wives close by whenever they're attempting to assemble anything. Who else can answer those tough questions like, "Where's my hammer?" "What'd you do with my screwdriver?" and "Why can't I ever find my tools when I need them?"

After they've worked until the wee hours of the morning to complete the project, who else but a loving wife would have the nerve to point out those three screws and two nuts that are always left over? (No matter what the project, there are always three screws and two nuts left over. Assemble a bike, there are three screws and two nuts left over. Build a doll house, there are three screws and two nuts left over. Personally, I think it's some sort of sick packaging joke.)

In spite of the instructions and the leftover parts, my husband somehow had the swing set up and operational just before dawn broke over the horizon. It was beautiful. A monument to parental perserverance. As soon as the children woke up, we tricked them into going outside. They saw the swing set and were so excited, they stayed out there playing on it for hours.

Now, this story would have remained a warm, wonderful Christmas memory if it weren't for one little fact. That year we also bought our sons their own tool boxes, each complete with hammer, socket wrench, screwdriver, and more.

While my husband and I were busy making a holiday fire out of all the empty boxes and wrapping paper, the boys had their own little project going. The swing set and tool set together proved to be too much of a temptation, and on one of our trips outside to check on them, we discovered that they had dismantled the entire thing! And they didn't even need the directions to do it.

All the pieces were lying in a pile in the middle of the sandbox, and the boys were standing ever so proudly next to them. It was one of those moments when you don't know whether to laugh, cry, applaud their mechanical skills, or return the tool set to the store before they knock out a wall and add a rumpus room to the house.

We opted to laugh about it. Besides, Dad could put it back together again. By now, he was an expert at reading the directions.

"The directions!" my husband screamed, racing to the fireplace just in time to see them swallowed up in flames.

The kids are all grown up now, but Dad still works on it every weekend.

"Now let's see… that was *insert A into B….*"

Questionable Behavior

Mary, Mary, quite contrary,
How does your garden grow?
And why is your name "Mary, Mary"?
That's what I'd like to know!

"I don't know… some days I just feel a little boxed in."

Children wonder about a lot of things:

Where does the sun go at night?
Why does it rain?
What makes a car go?
Why can't I take out my teeth like Uncle Henry?

Being inquisitive is a good thing, and usually our answers to questions of this variety don't cost us anything but time.

It's those questions accompanied by more expensive price tags that can get us down. Here are a few of the more costly questions, along with their estimated costs:

Why can't I have a red ant farm?

$90.00	for exterminator after red ants stage daring escape.
1.98	for one bag of infested sugar, discarded.
6.98	for book on red ants to replace the real thing.

Why can't I give my baby sister a haircut?

$20.00	for professional haircut to restyle Baby Sister's hair. (That "Moe" cut just doesn't become her.)
2.10	for eyebrow pencil to fill in missing brow from slip of hair clippers.
80.00	for counseling session after recurring Three Stooges dream.

Why can't I play with Mommy's purse?

$10.00	for new checkbook after bank informs you it can't accept checks written in lipstick.
45.00	for locksmith to replace your missing car keys.
75.00	for x-ray to determine if baby swallowed pennies in coin purse or merely stashed them for her college fund.

Why won't a tennis ball flush?

$20.00	for plumbing snake so Dad can remove ball.
135.00	for professional plumber to remove ball after Dad floods entire first floor of home.
85.00	to post lifeguard until water subsides.

Why can't I dry my teddy bear in the microwave?

$28.00	for new teddy bear.
15.00	to refill fire extinguisher.
2.00	for air freshener to cover aroma of "smoked" teddy.

Why don't dogs like wearing makeup?

$26.00	for new makeup kit.
2.00	for bar of dog soap.
120.00	for animal behavior therapy.

Why can't I play football in the house?

$120.00	to replace broken lamp.
226.00	to replace broken coffee table.
1,868.00	to fly in Dallas Cowboys scout to check out Baby's quarterbacking skills.

Why can't I drink fruit punch in my new white dress?

$15.00	to dry clean dress.
65.00	to shampoo carpets.
28.00	for throw rug to cover carpet stain that won't come out.

The goldfish looks hungry. Why can't I pour the whole box of fish food in the aquarium?

$13.46	for new goldfish.
2.54	for new box of fish food.
.33	burial expenses (3 flushes).

What's the biggest picture ever colored with crayons?

$150.00	to repaint living room walls.
100.00	for new curtains (the new paint made the old curtains look tacky).
1.98	for box of *washable* crayons.

Do you think I could have a raise in my allowance?

Price varies. Proceed with caution.

Free Wheelin'

Twinkle, Twinkle, Little Car,
I love to watch you roll so far.
I'll play with you and won't get bored
'Cause you're one car I can afford.

The rules of the contest had been set. Each boy was to make his own race car out of a block of wood.

The entrants were free to design their car any way they desired, but they couldn't solicit any help from dad, mom, older brother, uncle, grandfather, Manny, Moe, or Jack. All work had to be their own. No private investigators would be hired to make sure the rules were followed. Each boy was on the honor system.

Looking back now, hiring a couple of undercover detectives might not have been such a bad idea. The way some of the cars turned out, it not only appeared as though their relatives had assisted, it looked like a few car manufacturers did, too.

Our son made his own car. He sanded down the sides, painted it, complete with racing stripe and contest number, then attached the wheels. The finished product wasn't as flashy as the other cars in the competition, but at least our son could look those judges square in the eye and vow that every inch of that vehicle was his very own handiwork.

I'm not so sure that could be said about Randy Beaumont's car. Randy and his dad had a knack for winning at everything. They won the kite-flying contest every March, the potato-sack race each Fourth of July, the costume competition at the annual Harvest Party, and now it looked as though they were a shoe-in for the race car trophy.

Randy's vehicle was incredible. When he carried it into the scout meeting room that night there was a collective gasp from all the other competitors and their families. The design was awesome, each curve impeccably crafted, the chrome detail blinding. No one else's car stood a chance.

"You built that all by yourself?" one of the dads asked suspiciously.

"Yep," Randy nodded, polishing a hubcap.

"You didn't have any help?"

"Nope."

Another dad got in on the interrogation.

"That moon roof?" he noted. "You put that in yourself?"

"Yep."

"And the soda bar?"

"Uh-huh."

"Windshield wipers, cruise control, AM/FM stereo, cassette player—are you *sure* no one helped you?" he pressed.

"Positive," Randy insisted.

I don't think anyone believed him, but the kid was a rock. Not even Columbo could have gotten a confession out of him.

"Well..." the first dad sighed. "All I can say is you've got quite a future in the automobile industry."

"This is nothing," Randy smiled, proudly. "You should see my mobile home. I would have brought it tonight, but it's being rented out for the summer to a family of six."

None of us were sure if he was joking or telling the truth. But we didn't have time to worry about it. The judges announced that the race was about to begin.

Randy's car, otherwise known as Number 7, and four others were in the first race. They were instructed to place their cars on the ramp and await the starting signal. Tension filled the room as the leaders wished all the boys good luck.

The moment the flag went down, the boys let go of their cars and they were off. It was no surprise to anyone when Number 7 was the clear cut winner.

The second race saw Kevin McDonald's car, Number 5, take the lead early and maintain it all the way across the finish line.

Even though it lacked the flash of the other competitors, and its right rear wheel came off after the competition, Number 12, our son's car, took the third race.

It was time now for the finals. Our son reattached his wheel just as the judges were calling for the three top cars—Numbers 5, 7, and 12—to be placed on the starting line.

When each car was in place, the flag was dropped, and the final race to determine who would be the ultimate winner was in progress. Number 5 quickly took the lead, with Number 7 following in close pursuit. Number 12 gained some downhill momentum and was closing in. Without warning Number 5 began to stall, forfeiting the lead to Number 7. Number 12 began picking up more speed. The crowd exploded with excitement. Number 12 rolled closer and closer to Number 7. It was to be a photo finish for sure.

Then it happened. Number 12 began to wobble. Its body shimmied and its right rear wheel came off again, rolling off the track.

Its left front wheel disengaged, and rolled off the opposite side of the track. Amazingly enough, though, the car continued toward the finish line. The entire room watched anxiously to see who would win the coveted trophy.

Our hearts sank when, within a foot of the finish line, Number 12's front right wheel came off, leaving the car stalled on the track. But wait. The wheel didn't stop. It kept right on rolling and rolling and made a wobbly trek right over the finish line, seconds ahead of Number 7.

"You did it!" my husband shouted, picking up our son and swinging him around in celebration. "You did it! You won by a wheel!"

Unfortunately, the judges didn't agree. They had some rule about the *whole* car having to make it across the finish line to qualify, and Number 7 was awarded the winning trophy instead.

Our son still felt pretty good, though. Ol' Number 12 had completed the race (or at least part of it had), and that alone made it a winner!

Where's the Fire?

My kids once threw a tantrum.
They screamed and kicked their feet,
When I told them I'd cook dinner
Instead of going out to eat.

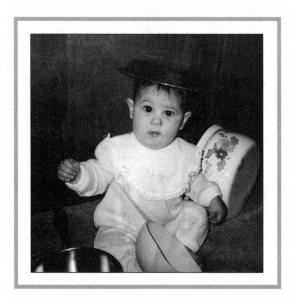

"I gotta quit watching those cooking shows."

One of our family traditions is to go out to eat at a nice restaurant every Christmas Eve. After all the shopping, all the wrapping, all the hustle bustle of the crowds, it's a treat to sit down and enjoy an evening of fine dining.

One year we decided to try a new restaurant that had just opened in town. We had heard a lot of good reports, and wanted to check it out for ourselves.

Upon our arrival the maitre d' welcomed us, led us to our table, and proceeded to describe the specialties of the house. One such specialty intrigued my husband—a choice of chicken, shrimp, or beef that we'd cook ourselves on a heated stone at our table.

"Why don't we try it?" he coaxed. "Sounds fun."

"You take me out to a nice restaurant, and I *still* have to cook?" I whined.

"It's all right, honey," he said. "It'll be supervised. Besides, restaurants always keep fire extinguishers on hand."

The kids cast their votes in Dad's favor, and it was now a closed matter. We were going to be cooking our own dinners, and paying $15.95 apiece for the pleasure.

It wasn't long before the waiter brought out our heated stone and placed it in the middle of our table. Setting the tray of meat beside it, he smiled and said, "Enjoy!" before disappearing into the kitchen.

Since it was his idea, my husband was the first to place his chicken on the stone tablet.

"Shouldn't it be sizzling?" I asked, after five minutes of watching nothing much happen.

"Maybe it's cooking internally," he reasoned. "You know, like a microwave."

We threw on some shrimp just to see how they would fare. They, too, sat there.

"Are you sure the tablet's hot enough?" I asked.

He carefully put his finger on the stone. Then two fingers. Then his whole hand, which didn't sizzle any more than the chicken had. We asked for a different stone, but it wasn't much better. At the rate we were going, the meat was going to spoil before it cooked.

When it became obvious that the only thing getting hot was my husband's collar, we decided to review our options.

"We could ask for a third stone," I said, grilling a slice of beef over our centerpiece candle.

"We could change our order," the boys suggested.

"We could go somewhere else to eat," was my husband's recommendation, and once again it received the most votes.

We paid our bill, had the valet bring up our car, and drove to another restaurant about two blocks away. We could smell the aroma of sizzling beef as we pulled into their driveway. They didn't have valet parking, and we weren't going to be eating by candlelight. But they *did* cook our meat for us. And anyway, that glow from their golden arches gave the evening a certain festive feeling after all.

Little Shop(ping Trip) of Horrors

Shopping trips with Junior
Can be grueling, heaven knows—
Especially playing "hid and seek'
In circular racks of clothes!

Grocery store shopping carts now come with infant seats, seat belts, and ride-along seats for older siblings. The only thing they still need to invent is a set of blinders that parents can put on their children before heading down the toy, cookie, or ice cream aisles. Children can pick up the scent of the Hostess display eight aisles away. (The best I can do is four aisles.)

It's not easy to shop with kids. They can triple your grocery tab, and leave you wondering how in the world they managed to talk you into paying $4.50 for a box of cereal that nobody in the house likes just because there's a three-cent toy inside!

In recent years, some grocery stores have begun offering "temptation free" check-out lanes. These lanes have nothing on display to tempt children—no candy bars, gum, or toys. (Frankly, I think they should have something like that for us adults. Perhaps a check-out lane with *only* milk and bread for all those times when we stop in for only milk and bread, but leave with two carts full!)

Shopping for clothes with children can present its own share of problems. Most children have a three-rack attention span. After that, they start finding other ways to entertain themselves. This might include (but is not limited to) making goofy faces in the mirrors, doing the "Mommy, pick me up" dance, and announcing they have to go to the bathroom just as soon as you finally nab that dressing room after a twenty-minute wait.

There is an advantage, though, to taking along a toddler on our shopping trips. At grocery stores, they fill up the little seat, thus keeping us from buying that many more groceries, and forcing us to stay within our budget. At bakeries and jewelry stores you get waited on faster... especially if their glass display windows have just been cleaned. And at department stores, when two shoppers see a blouse at the same time from across the aisle and race toward it, the one with the stroller usually wins.

Exercising Parental Rights

Jack B. Worn Out
Jack B. Sore
Jack B. Exhausted
When the day is o'er.

"Sure, I'll meet you at high noon, Black Bart... just as soon as I learn how to tell time."

It's difficult for most parents of toddlers to find time for a regular exercise routine. However, throughout the day they do manage to burn off plenty of calories in other ways. Because most parents don't realize how much exercise they really *are* getting, the following table is provided.

Parents of Toddlers' Daily Exercise Chart

One-legged hop (after baby rolls over your other foot with his walker)   *Calories burned - 60 per episode*

Knee bends (cleaning up spilt milk)
Calories burned - 4 per bend

Twenty-six-mile marathon (chasing toddler at bath time)   *Calories burned - 340*

Playing Patty-Cake (278 times a day)
Calories burned - 450

Standing broad jump (to intercept ball thrown by toddler in direction of irreplaceable antique lamp)
Calories burned - 48

Fifty-yard dash (to get telephone away from toddler who just answered it and is proceeding to hang up on caller)   *Calories burned - 63*

Twenty-eight laps around obstacle course of toys left on floor each day   *Calories burned - 358*

Push-ups (to get out of bed at 4 A.M. to get toddler a drink of water)   *Calories burned - 37*

Bench-pressing 30 pounds (whenever toddler wants to be carried)   *Calories burned - 8 per lift*

Arm stretches around toddler (otherwise known as hugs)   *Calories burned - less than 4 per hug**

*It's been proven, however, that *this* exercise gets the *best* results.

Fish Stories

Row, row, row your boat,
Catch a fish today.
And keep your story straight about
The one that got away.

"Sushi, anyone?"

Father-son (or father-daughter) fishing trips are a great way to develop family closeness. Catching the fish, frying it up, and eating it together—it doesn't get any better than that.

Now, any fisherman worth his salt can tell you stories about "the one that got away"—that Moby-esque catch of a lifetime that was very nearly snagged using only one anemic worm and extraordinary fishing skills.

My husband, an avid fisherman, has more fish tales than Mrs. Paul. He's caught bass, catfish, shark, seaweed, and enough empty soda cans to make our house payment for three months. He even taught each of our sons to fish. I have never quite mastered the sport myself. I don't come back with stories about the *fish* that got away. I return with stories about the *fishing pole* that got away.

That's why I usually let father and son go on their outings alone. They bring back the fish and I burn it. It just works better that way. There was that one time, though, when my husband got a little *too* excited over one of their catches.

"Now, *this* beauty deserves to be mounted," he said proudly, holding up the fish.

"That's lovely, dear," I commented, underwhelmed. "But hardly worth mounting. How about a nice key chain instead?"

"Are you kidding? This baby needs to be where

everyone can see it!" he said, beaming. "You know, like professional fishermen do."

"You're not really going to call a taxidermist for *that*, are you?" I asked.

He shook his head. "I'm not trusting this prize catch to a taxidermist. Besides, who knows what they'd charge? I'll do it myself."

And with that, he headed for the garage.

Recalling the garbage disposal he repaired himself (at four times the cost of a professional plumber) and the washing machine he helped to run more quietly (after he worked on it, it never ran again), I decided I'd better follow.

"Have you ever done anything like this before?" I asked as he laid the fish on his work table.

"No," he shrugged. "But how hard could it be?"

The first step was to gut the fish. That seemed logical enough. Gutting it, though, made that poor critter lose what little fullness it had. It now appeared almost two-dimensional, so he decided to plump it up with pieces of newspaper.

After the fish had all the news he could stomach (I know the feeling), he was ready to be preserved. My husband mounted him onto a board using various brackets and hooks. Then, taking a can of resin from the shelf, he proceeded to baste that poor fish into posterity. Five coats of resin later that fish was destined to be with us forever.

Unfortunately, so was the smell.

With each passing day, we became more and more aware of the fact that resin doesn't lock in odor. For three years our house had the lovely aroma of a fish cannery. Summers were the worst. Those 104-degree days do wonders for aged trout.

After one particularly grueling heat wave, I managed to talk my husband into taking a final picture (Kodak memories don't smell) before tossing out the shriveled-up souvenir. After all, it was the humane thing to do for the poor fish... and for everyone within a three-mile radius of our house. Besides, the fish had begun to look like an elongated prune with eyes.

But that was all right. Both my husband and my son knew there were plenty of other fish in the sea. And even though that pungent souvenir of their fishing trip was finally gone, the memory of their time together was sure to last forever.

Romance on the Run

Since Baby came, it seems romance
Has really had to suffer.
We would kiss, but both of us
Are much too tired to pucker!

With a toddler in the house, it's not easy for parents to find time for romance. They have to steal a hug in the hallway, a kiss in the kitchen, a wink in the washroom. If this sounds familiar, don't despair. There are ways to ensure romance stays in your lives. You just have to be a little more creative.

Here are a few hints:

- Cuddle up on a bearskin rug in front of the fireplace (if bearskin rug is not available, substitute Winnie-the-Pooh quilt).

- Go for a stroll in the sandbox and pretend you're walking along the beach together.

- Play romantic music (preferably nothing involving chipmunks or purple dinosaurs).

- Hike the pile of dirty laundry together. Pack a picnic lunch, taking plenty of water and two clothespins for your noses.

- Enjoy a romantic candlelight dinner (removing food from styrofoam containers first to minimize fire hazard).

- Leave a romantic message on Baby's Fisher-Price tape recorder.

- Toast each other with a glass of chocolate milk.

- Read a poem to each other that doesn't involve a mother named Goose or a cat in headwear.

- Bring your wife a dozen roses. She'll thank you for it, and the scent will help cover up that pungent diaper pail odor.

- Fall asleep in each other's arms (but preferably *not* while hugging on your front porch).

- Finally, engage in plenty of pillow talk other than: "The baby's crying. It's *your* turn to feed and change her."
  "It's *your* turn."
  "It's *your* turn."
  "It's *your...*"

However you plan those romantic moments together, the important thing is to make sure you have them. Because becoming a *family* doesn't mean you cease being a *couple*.

Stroller Messages

How could I get a ticket?
I'm still too young to read.
It's not *my* fault my stroller
Picked up some downhill speed.

"But officer, I *wasn't*
speeding—honest!"

Cars have them. Motorcycles have them. Bicycles have them. So, why not strollers? What are they? Bumper stickers. When you think about it, we all need a place to let the world know where we stand on the issues. A baby isn't any different. I can see it now—the rear bumper of strollers the world over will soon be covered with deep, thought-provoking messages like:

I teethe, therefore I am.

Thumbsucking—it's not just for breakfast anymore.

Reach out and burp someone.

My other car is a walker.

If you can read this,
thank Mother Goose.

My mom was an honor
student in Lamaze class.

Save the storks.

Have a *dry* day.

I brake for all toy sales.

How am I driving?

Call 1-800-2PushMe.

The end is near
(of my bottle)!

It's 10 o'clock. Do you know where your teddy is?

Eat puréed.

Babies Against Naps.

I ♥ my pacifier.

Got formula?

Drooler on board.

Have you hugged your parents today?

Now I Lay Me Down to Sleep

Now I lay me down to sleep.
My mommy says I should count sheep.
But I don't know what I should do,
'Cause I can only count to two!

Bedtime. Sometimes you tuck your children into bed and they're fast asleep before you can tiptoe out of the room. Other times it requires three bedtime stories, a glass of water, six crackers, two calls to Grandma, fourteen lullabies, and a bedtime prayer.

My favorite part of this nightime ritual is the bedtime prayer. I love listening to children pray. They're so sincere... they just tell it like it is, even when they do a rewrite of an old favorite such as:

> *Now I lay me down to nap,*
> *I'm quite content on Daddy's lap.*
> *But if you hear an awful roaring,*
> *Don't panic—it's just Daddy snoring.*

Children's prayers can be so charmingly sincere, wonderfully innocent, and profound. When my husband and I were teaching children's church, there was a little girl who prayed every Sunday for several months for a burning house that she saw on her way to church. Now, unless the lady of the house went to the same cooking school I did, I'm sure the firemen weren't battling a blaze there every Sunday morning. Still, this little girl prayed weekly for the structure to stop burning. If you ever had a need, that little girl would be the person you'd want praying for you. Talk about perseverance!

I have to say, though, that the most memorable prayer I ever heard a child pray came from my middle son, Matt. I had only been hired as a writer for Bob

Hope for several months when one night after praying his usual prayer, Matt added this little closing: "And God, thank You for Mommy, Daddy, our dog Chipper, our cat, my pet hamster, and thanks, Lord, for the memories."